A Kid's Guide to Drawing America™

How to Draw
Oklahoma's
Sights and Symbols

Eric Fein

OBSOLETE

The Rosen Publishing Group's
PowerKids Press™
New York

Published in 2002 by The Rosen Publishing Group, Inc.
29 East 21st Street, New York, NY 10010

First Edition

Editors: Jennifer Landau, Jennifer Way
Book Design: Kim Sonsky
Layout Design: Michael Donnellan

Illustration Credits: Emily Muschinske
Photo Credits: p. 7 © Index Stock; p. 8 © The Wichita Eagle; p. 9 © The Philbrook Museum of Art, Tulsa, Oklahoma; pp. 12, 14 © One Mile Up, Incorporated; p. 16 © Clay Perry/CORBIS; p. 18 © Richard Hamilton Smith/CORBIS; p. 20 © Tim Zurowski/CORBIS; p. 22 © Doug Wechsler; p. 24 © Christie's Images/CORBIS; pp. 26, 28 © Danny Lehman/CORBIS.

Fein, Eric
        How to draw Oklahoma's sights and symbols / Eric Fein.
            p. cm. — (A kid's guide to drawing America)
        Includes index.
        Summary: This book explains how to draw some of Oklahoma's sights and symbols, including the state seal and the official flower.
        ISBN 0-8239-6092-7
        1. Emblems, State—Oklahoma—Juvenile literature 2. Oklahoma—In art—Juvenile literature
3. Drawing—Technique—Juvenile literature [1. Emblems, State—Oklahoma 2. Oklahoma
3. Drawing—Technique] I. Title II. Series
        2002
        743'.8'99766—dc21

CONTENTS

Let's Draw Oklahoma

Oklahoma is a state with a lot of variety, both physically and culturally. The state has mountainous areas and areas of flat, dry plains. Oklahoma is also home to more than 67 Native American groups.

Oklahoma is an agricultural leader, ranking fourth in the country in wheat production and in cattle production.

Oklahoma has 50 state parks. The Chickasaw National Recreation Area is in the Arbuckle Mountains. These mountains are known for their springs, which produce mineral water.

Black Mesa State Park is known for its pictographs of the pre-Columbian Plains Native Americans. Pictographs are ancient drawings done on rocks.

Oklahoma City is home to the National Cowboy and Western Heritage Museum. This museum houses a re-creation of an Old West town called Prosperity Junction. The museum also features the Rodeo Hall of Fame.

This book will help you draw some of Oklahoma's most interesting sights and symbols. Each chapter has step-by-step instructions on how to draw that chapter's subject. The drawings are broken down into several easy-to-follow steps. Each new drawing step is shown in red. As you draw, you will learn the proper names and terms for the drawing shapes and tools you will use.

You will need the following supplies to draw Oklahoma's sights and symbols:

- A sketch pad
- An eraser
- A number 2 pencil
- A pencil sharpener

These are some of the shapes and drawing terms you need to know to draw Oklahoma's sights and symbols:

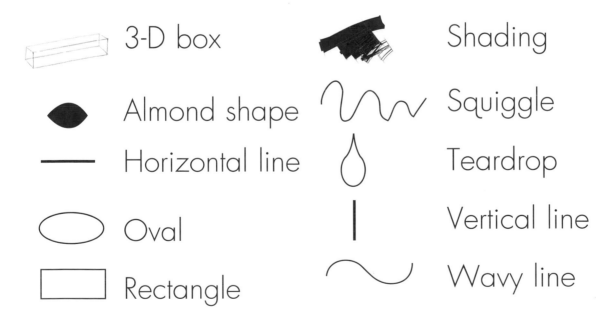

3-D box

Almond shape

Horizontal line

Oval

Rectangle

Shading

Squiggle

Teardrop

Vertical line

Wavy line

The Sooner State

Oklahoma got its name from two Choctaw words. *Okla* means "people." *Homma* means "red." Oklahoma is home to the largest Native American population in the United States. More than 250,000 Native Americans live in Oklahoma.

Most of Oklahoma was bought by the United States as part of the Louisiana Purchase in 1803. In 1834, land was set aside for the Native Americans. By 1889, the government had been pressured into opening up these lands for white settlers. The government decided to have people line up at the border and wait for a signal to be given. After the signal, the settlers could race into the territory to claim land. Some settlers sneaked into the territory before the race started. They were called Sooners. This is why Oklahoma is known as the Sooner State.

On November 16, 1907, Oklahoma joined the United States and became the forty-sixth state. Oklahoma City is the state capital and the most populated city in the state.

Oklahoma is rich in Native American history. This Kiowa chief in Anadarko, Oklahoma, is a member of 1 of more than 60 Native American nations that populate Oklahoma.

Oklahoma Artist

Blackbear Bosin

Native American artist Blackbear Bosin was born on June 5, 1921, in Anadarko, Oklahoma. Bosin's first look at the work of Native American artists was when he went to Saint Patrick's Mission School in Anadarko. His style was influenced most by a group of Native American artists known as the Kiowa Five. The Kiowa Five painted to preserve images of their Native American history and customs that were beginning to disappear. The Kiowa Five painted with vivid, flat colors and used no shadows or perspective in their pictures.

Bosin was inspired by the Kiowa Five paintings and taught himself how to paint. Like the Kiowa Five, Bosin painted flat, solidly colored designs. In this style of painting, it is more important to capture the feeling of a landscape than to show it as it actually appears. Bosin usually used gouache for painting. Gouache is a kind of opaque, or cloudy, watercolor paint. Bosin's paintings show images of his Plains ancestors.

During World War II (1939–1945), Bosin served as a soldier in the U.S. Marine Corps. He had his first one-man art show in Honolulu, Hawaii, in 1945. After the war, he began to show his work throughout the United States. His work was displayed in the White House and in the National Gallery of Art in Washington, D.C. Bosin died on August 9, 1980.

© *Prairie Fire*, c. 1953, Francis Blackbear Bosin, Kiowa-Comanche, 1921–1980, Gouache on brown paper, Museum purchase, The Philbrook Museum of Art, Tulsa, Oklahoma. 1953.7

Bosin's 1953 painting *Prairie Fire* shows the influence of the artwork of the Kiowa Five painters. This painting is done in gouache on brown paper and measures 23" x 33 ⅛" (58 cm x 84 cm).

Map of Oklahoma

Map of the Continental United States

Oklahoma is the eighteenth-largest state in the United States. It covers an area of 69,903 square miles (181,048 sq km). Its highest point is Black Mesa, which is 4,973 feet (1,516 m) above sea level. Oklahoma's lowest point is along the Little River in McCurtain County. This area is 287 feet (87 m) above sea level.

Oklahoma is bordered by six states. Colorado and Kansas lie to Oklahoma's north. Missouri and Arkansas are to the east. Texas lies to the south and the west of Oklahoma, and on the western tip of Oklahoma's panhandle is New Mexico. Oklahoma has four mountain ranges: the Ouachitas, the Arbuckles, the Wichitas, and the Kiamichis.

1

Oklahoma can be drawn using very simple shapes. Begin with a rectangle.

2

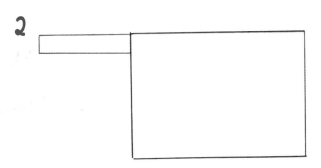

Add a thin rectangle to the left side, like the handle on a pot.

3

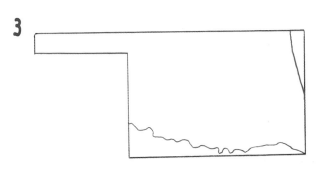

Add a wavy line to the bottom, or southern border, of the state. Add a curved line to the right border.

4

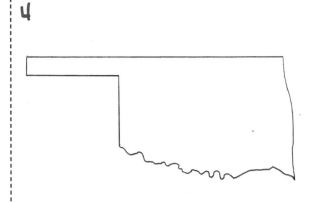

Erase extra lines.

5

Black Mesa

Indian City U.S.A.

Lake Murray

Oklahoma City

Tulsa

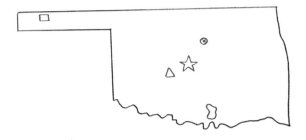

a. Draw a rectangle for Black Mesa.
b. Draw a triangle for Indian City U.S.A.
c. Draw a squiggle oval for Lake Murray.
d. Draw a star for Oklahoma City, the state's capital.
e. Draw a circle with a dot in it for Tulsa.

The State Seal

Oklahoma's state seal features a large, five-pointed star. This large star is surrounded by 45 smaller stars, which represent the 45 states that made up the country when Oklahoma became a state in 1907. In the center of the star is the seal that was used when Oklahoma was a territory. This image shows a settler and a Native American shaking hands. It represents a wish for both groups to live peacefully in Oklahoma. In each point of the star is an emblem of one of the Five Civilized Tribes of Oklahoma.

The term Five Civilized Tribes was created by European Americans and refers to the Cherokee, the Chickasaw, the Choctaw, the Creek, and the Seminole groups. It wasn't until 1901 that all the members of the Five Civilized Tribes were made U.S. citizens.

1

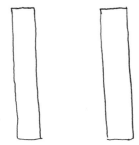

For this drawing, we will focus on the section of the seal that shows a Native American man and a pioneer shaking hands. The basic shape of each figure is a rectangle.

2

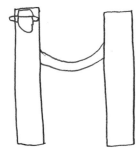

Begin with the pioneer's head. Notice that he's wearing a cowboy hat. Draw the *U*-shaped form that will be your guide as you draw their hands shaking.

3

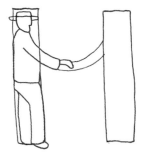

Add the body of the pioneer. His arm reaches out in front of him in the *U*-shaped arc.

4

Draw the Native American's head. He wears a headdress that drops down his back.

5

Add the simple outlines of the Native American's chest, arms, pants, and moccasins.

6

Erase extra lines. Draw a triangle with three lines on top of it behind the Native American. This represents his home, a tepee.

7

Now add the train engine behind the pioneer. Follow the shapes in the picture. This represents the railroad that pioneers built on the land where the Native American people lived.

8

Add shading and detail, and you are done.

The State Flag

Oklahoma has had two official state flags. The first was used from 1911 to 1925. In 1924, Oklahoma's legislature felt it was time for a flag that represented the different cultures that existed in Oklahoma. The legislature held a contest. Louise Fluke, an artist, won.

This winning design was made the official state flag on April 2, 1925. It honors Native Americans and their ancestors. The flag has a sky-blue background. In the center is an Osage battle shield. Seven eagle feathers hang from the bottom of the shield. There are six crosses on the face of the shield. Crossed over the shield are a Native American peace pipe, or calumet, and an olive branch. In 1941, "Oklahoma" was added to the bottom of the flag.

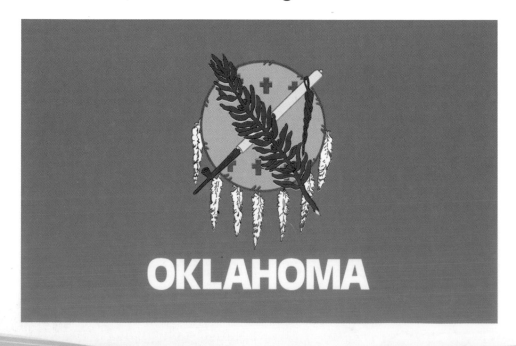

1

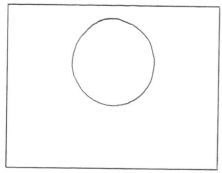

Draw a large rectangle. Add a circle in the middle of the rectangle. This will be the outline of the shield.

2

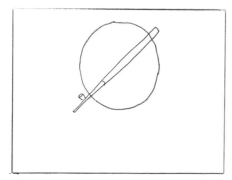

Add the pipe. It is made using diagonal lines and is shaped like a skinny baseball bat.

3

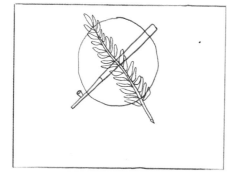

Draw the branch. First draw the long, diagonal stem. Then add oval leaves on each side of the stem.

4

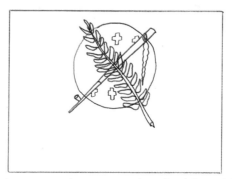

Draw the cross shapes on the shield. Add the outline of the feather that hangs from the pipe.

5

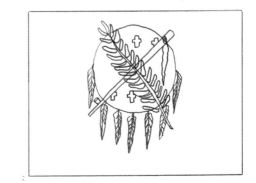

Add seven feathers hanging from the shield.

6

Add shading and detail. Print the word "OKLAHOMA" at the bottom of your flag, and you are done.

The Mistletoe Plant

Oklahoma was the second state to choose a state flower. This event took place at the 1893 World's Fair in Chicago. Each of the states was invited to select an official flower to represent their state at the fair. The people of Oklahoma chose mistletoe (*Phoradendron serotinum*).

Mistletoe had been put on the graves of settlers as decoration when no other flowers were available.

The mistletoe plant is a parasite. This means it lives on other plants or trees. Mistletoe has tiny yellow flowers and forked branches. Mistletoe produces seeded white berries that are poisonous both to people and to animals.

Mistletoe is used as a decoration during the holiday season. The custom of kissing under the mistletoe began in England. It was believed that kissing while standing under mistletoe would lead to marriage.

1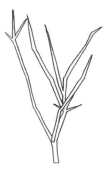

Begin by outlining the mistletoe branch using many crooked *V*-shapes of different sizes.

2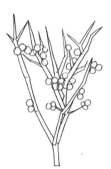

Add a few more stems coming off the main branches. Draw circles for the mistletoe berries on some of the branches.

3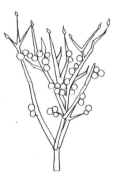

Erase extra lines where the berries and the branches overlap. Add a tiny teardrop shape to the tip of each of the tallest stems. These will become the leaves.

4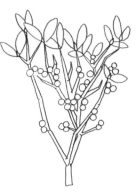

Add almond-shaped leaves. Notice that there are two leaves, like rabbit ears, on the top of each of the highest stems.

5

Shade your drawing. Shade lightly at the edges. Good work!

The Redbud

Redbuds (*Cercis canadensis*) are found throughout Oklahoma. They grow in forests, in valleys, and on hillsides. For the early settlers, redbuds added cheery colors to land that was harsh and dreary. Maimee Lee Robinson was a conservationist. She came to Oklahoma in 1922, and immediately fell in love with the beauty of the redbud. She formed a committee to get the Oklahoma legislature to make the redbud the official state tree. She succeeded. The redbud was named Oklahoma's state tree on March 30, 1937.

Redbuds are small trees that usually grow to be about 15 feet (4.5 m) tall and 15 feet (4.5 m) wide. Redbud leaves are heart shaped or round. The leaves start out bronze colored and then turn green. In the fall, they turn yellow. The flowers of a redbud are dark brown buds that bloom into pink-lavender flowers in the spring.

1

Draw two lines for the trunk. Notice how the trunk gets a little wider right near the ground.

2

Add branches reaching up.

3

Add more branches coming out of the first set of branches. These might be a bit thinner. Notice how they form Y shapes.

4

Add lines coming out of the thinner branches. These are the thinnest branches.

5

Draw a wavy, fluffy shape around the branches. This will be the leafy area.

6

Shade the trunk and the branches dark. The bark has a lot of repeated vertical lines.

7

Shade the leafy area by drawing lots of little, squiggly lines. Hold your pencil loosely in your hand and shake it back and forth to make these kinds of marks.

The Scissor-Tailed Flycatcher

Oklahoma approved the scissor-tailed flycatcher, or scissortail, as its official state bird on May 26, 1951. Many bird lovers and scientists pushed to have the scissortail made the state bird, because Oklahoma is right in the middle of the bird's nesting range.

The bird gets its name from its scissor-shaped tail. Scissor-tailed flycatchers can be from 11 to 15 inches (28–38 cm) long. Female scissortails are usually shorter than males, because they have shorter tails. The wings of a scissortail are black with bright red at the shoulders. The undersides of the wings are pale pink. Scissor-tailed flycatchers help Oklahoma farmers, because the birds eat insects that ruin crops, such as grasshoppers and crickets.

Begin with a circle for the bird's head.

2

Add a triangle for the beak.

3

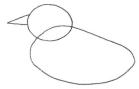

Add a wide oval for the bird's body.

4

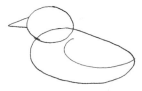

Draw a curved shape for the wing.

5

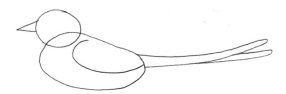

Draw two tail feathers. These feathers make the bird different from other birds. They look like scissors.

6

Add the bird's eye and leg.

7

Add a perch, or a branch for the bird to rest on. Shade the bird, paying attention to the markings on its feathers.

The Bullfrog

The bullfrog (*Rana catesbeiana*), the largest frog in the United States, was made Oklahoma's official state amphibian on May 5, 1997. Bullfrogs are found throughout Oklahoma. They have large ears, called tympana, located behind their eyes. Their tympana let them hear the calls of other bullfrogs. Bullfrogs' hind legs can be 10 inches (25 cm) long. Their feet are webbed. This means that skin grows between their toes. A bullfrog's feet look like swim fins. Bullfrogs can jump from 3 to 6 feet (1–2 m).

Bullfrogs are green or brown and can weigh about 1 pound (0.5 kg) or more. Their bellies are white or yellow. Bullfrogs live in or near bodies of still water, such as ponds. Bullfrogs eat anything that they can swallow, including birds, reptiles, fish, snakes, small turtles, and even other frogs.

1

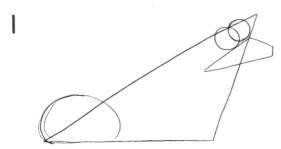

First outline the basic shapes of the bullfrog. Notice that the body is like a triangle, the rear leg is like an oval, the eyes are two circles, and the mouth is a triangle with a flat, cutoff edge.

2

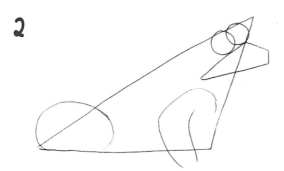

Add two curved lines for the front leg. Notice the bullfrog has a strong shoulder to help it to jump.

3

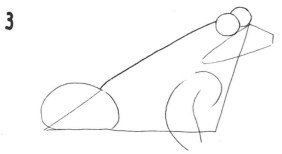

Now focus on the eyes. Erase the extra lines where the eyes overlap. Then look at the bullfrog's back. Redraw the line so that it has a curve all the way to the hind leg.

4

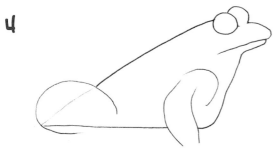

Redraw the mouth and the belly, erasing the triangular guides as you go.

5

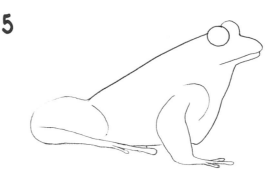

Redraw the front and the rear legs, adding long toes.

6

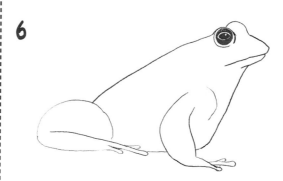

Add detail to the bullfrog's eye. Notice that there is a dark almond shape inside a white outline inside a dark circle. Look carefully at the picture for help.

7

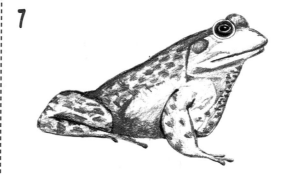

Shade. Use your pencil to create the look of the bullfrog's skin. Its skin is bumpy and spotted. Notice that the bullfrog has a dark, round spot on the side of its head. That's one of its ears, or tympana.

Fort Sill

On January 8, 1869, Major General Philip H. Sheridan claimed the land on which Camp Wichita was built. Sheridan and his troops were sent to keep the peace in the area. The Plains Indians, angry at being forced to give up their lands, began to leave their reservations to attack white settlements.

Sheridan changed the name from Camp Wichita to Fort Sill to honor his friend, Brigadier General Joshua W. Sill, who was killed during the Civil War. The fort covers 94,220 acres (38,129 ha) of land near Lawton, Oklahoma.

The great Chiricahua Apache warrior Geronimo fought so his people could keep their lands. He was captured in 1886 and was sent to Fort Sill. Geronimo died on February 17, 1909, while at Fort Sill.

1

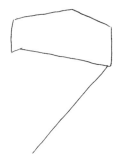

Begin by looking at the photograph. Draw a rough outline of Geronimo's head scarf using simple, straight lines. Then draw a long diagonal line for Geronimo's coat.

2

Draw a line through the head scarf to show that the scarf wraps around his head in layers. Then draw an arc to use as a guide as you draw Geronimo's face. Draw a small line for his neck.

3

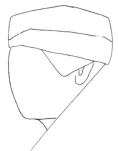

Draw a triangle for Geronimo's hair. He has it tucked behind his ear. Draw the ear using a curved line for the earlobe and a small curve for the ear hole.

4

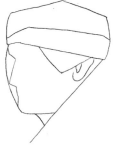

Now outline the side of Geronimo's face, or his profile. Use the arc as a guide as you outline his forehead, nose, mouth, and chin.

5

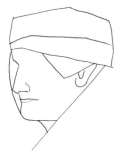

Add a line for his nostril and two lines for his lips.

6

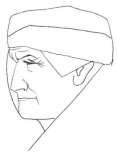

This picture of Geronimo was taken when he was old. His face has many lines from his time spent outside in the wind and the sun.

7

Add lines to Geronimo's hair to show that it is long, streaked black and gray, and tucked behind his ear into the scarf.

8

Shade your drawing, looking carefully at the photo. Notice the wrinkles on the top of his nose. Notice the lines in his cheek and the shadows under his nose and under his bottom lip. Notice that his neck is dark.

Indian City U.S.A.

Indian City U.S.A. is a large outdoor museum that gives people a realistic look at the way Native Americans from several places in the Southwest once lived. Indian City U.S.A. was organized by the citizens of Anadarko, Oklahoma.

Eight Native American nations are represented in Indian City U.S.A. These nations are the Navajo, the Chiracahua, the Apache, the Wichita, the Kiowa, the Caddo, the Pawnee, and the Pueblo. Each nation has a tribal village. There are many different items to see, including tools, baby cradles, cooking tools, weapons, and musical instruments. Native Americans lead visitors on guided tours and share information about Native American customs and beliefs.

1

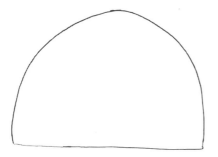

Let's draw a stick hut to represent Indian City U.S.A. First draw a dome, or a half circle shape.

2

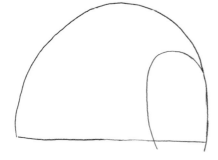

Add a horseshoe shape for the door.

3

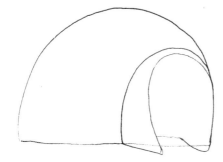

Add a larger horseshoe to create a doorway.

4

Erase extra lines.

5

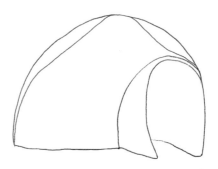

Make the top of the hut pointier. Erase the guide line.

6

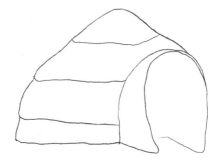

Divide the hut into sections using curved horizontal lines.

7

Shade the drawing. Create the look of the hut by repeating a lot of lines. Leave a light line between each section. This is the rope that holds the sticks to the hut.

Oklahoma's Capitol

The Oklahoma state capitol building is located in Oklahoma City, the state's capital city. Construction on the building began in 1914, and the capitol was opened in the summer of 1917.

Architects Solomon A. Layton and Wemyss Smith designed the building using Greco-Roman elements. Greco-Roman architecture is a combination of Greek and Roman architecture.

Oklahoma's capitol building is the only capitol in the world to be surrounded by working oil wells. The building is one of only 12 state capitol buildings that have no domes. A dome was originally planned for the building, but the builders ran out of money.

Begin with a rectangle to create the center section of the building.

2

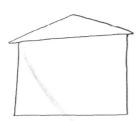

Add a flat triangle on top of the square.

3

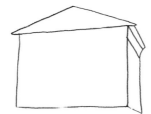

Add the right side of the center section of the capitol. This side slants away from you, so use diagonal lines.

4

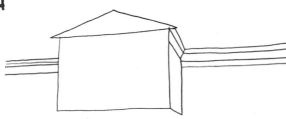

Add horizontal lines on each side of the center section.

5

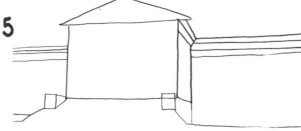

Draw the small platforms on the side of the front staircase using 3-D boxes. Add diagonal lines slanting downward from these platforms. Add the bottom edge of the right and left sections of the building.

6

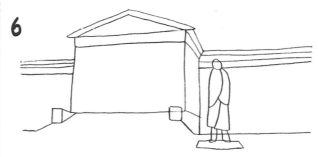

Add the outline of the statue in front of the building. This statue has a circle for a head. You can make this part by using simple curved shapes for the clothes and the body.

7

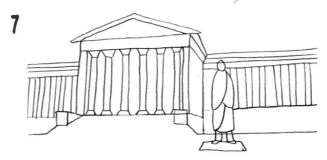

Add columns to the building.

8

Shade the drawing. Notice that the spaces between each column are dark and the columns are light, because sunlight hits them directly. Add horizontal lines to the stairs.

Oklahoma State Facts

Statehood	November 16, 1907, 46th state
Area	69,903 square miles (181,048 sq km)
Population	3,450,700
Capital	Oklahoma City, population, 469,900
Most Populated City	Oklahoma City
Industries	Transportation equipment, electric products, rubber and plastic products, oil, natural gas
Agriculture	Cattle, wheat, peanuts, pecans
Tree	Redbud
Game animal	American buffalo
Rock	Barite rose
Song	"Oklahoma"
Bird	Scissor-tailed flycatcher
Flower	Mistletoe
Amphibian	Bullfrog
Fish	White bass
Nickname	The Sooner State
Motto	Labor Conquers All Things
Reptile	Collared lizard

Glossary

agricultural (a-grih-KUL-cher-uhl) Having to do with farms or farming.

amphibian (am-FIH-bee-uhn) An animal that can live both in water and on land.

ancestors (AN-ses-turz) Relatives who lived long ago.

Civil War (SIH-vul WOR) The war fought between the northern and southern states of America from 1861 to 1865.

conservationist (kahn-ser-VAY-shun-ist) Someone who wants to preserve and to protect the lands, the wildlife, and other natural resources of a country.

Five Civilized Tribes (FYV SIH-vuh-lyzd TRYBZ) The name for the Chickasaw, Choctaw, Cherokee, Creek, and Seminole Native Americans. These groups adopted many European customs, which at the time were considered more civilized than Native American customs.

gouache (GWAHSH) A type of watercolor paint that is not transparent.

Greco-Roman (GREK-oh-roh-man) A style of architecture that uses elements from Greek architecture and Roman architecture.

legislature (LEH-jihs-lay-cher) A body of people that has the power to make or pass laws.

opaque (oh-PAYK) Not see-through.

panhandle (PAN-han-dl) A narrow projection of a larger territory.

parasite (PAR-eh-syt) An organism that lives on or in another type of organism and receives nutrients.

perspective (per-SPEK-tiv) The way in which a picture on a flat surface can show objects that seem to be at a distance.

reservations (reh-zer-VAY-shunz) Areas of land set aside by the government for Native Americans to live on.

sea level (SEE LEH-vul) A way to measure how high or low something is on Earth's surface.

technique (tek-NEEK) A method or way of bringing about a desired result in a science, an art, a sport, or a profession.

Index

Web Sites

To learn more about the people and places of Oklahoma, check out these Web sites:
www.state.ok.us/
www.50states.com/oklahoma.htm

OBSOLETE